CW01664262

Am I fat?

Jack's cat is sad.

Jack's cat is very sad.

I am very sad.

I am big and I am fat.

Jack's cat ran to the rat.

The rat sat on the mat.

Rat, Rat, am I fat?

Am I big and
am I fat?

Yes, very big
and very fat ...

but...

Jack's cat ran to the frog.

The frog sat on the log.

Frog, Frog, am I fat?

Am I big and am I fat?

Yes, very big and very fat ...

but...

Jack's cat ran to the pug.

The pug sat on the rug.

Pug, Pug, am I fat?

Am I big and am I fat?

Yes, very big
and very fat ...

but...

Jack's cat is sad.

Jack's cat is very sad.

Jack's cat went to the pig.

Pig, Pig, am I fat?
Am I big and am I fat?

Yes, but I like big, fat cats!
And I like big, fat pigs!

And we like big fat cats.
We like big fat cats a lot!